NATIONAL
GEOGRAPHIC

School Publishing

Measurement and Data

Rebecca Sabatani

PICTURE CREDITS

Illustrations by Marjory Gardner (4–5, 8–9, 10–11, 12–13, 14–15, 16).
Cover, 2, 6 (above right), 7 (all), 9 (above), APL/Corbis; 1, 6 (left), 16 (above left),
Lindsay Edwards Photography; 8 (all), 9 (below right), Getty Images; 10 (above right),
Keith Dannemiller/Alamy; 11, Photolibrary.com.

Produced through the worldwide resources of the National Geographic Society,
John M. Fahey, Jr., President and Chief Executive Officer; Gilbert M. Grosvenor,
Chairman of the Board; Nina D. Hoffman, Executive Vice President and President,
Books and Education Publishing Group.

PREPARED BY NATIONAL GEOGRAPHIC SCHOOL PUBLISHING

Ericka Markman, Senior Vice President and President Children's Books and Education
Publishing Group; Steve Mico, Senior Vice President and Publisher; Marianne Hiland,
Editorial Director; Lynnette Brent, Executive Editor; Michael Murphy and Barbara Wood,
Senior Editors; Bea Jackson, Design Director; David Dumo, Art Director; Margaret
Sidlowsky, Illustrations Director; Matt Wascavage, Manager of Publishing Services;
Sean Philpotts, Production Manager.

MANUFACTURING AND QUALITY MANAGEMENT

Christopher A. Liedel, Chief Financial Officer; Phillip L. Schlosser, Director;
Clifton M. Brown III, Manager.

BOOK DEVELOPMENT

Ibis for Kids Australia Pty Limited.

Published by the National Geographic Society
1145 17th Street, N.W.
Washington, D.C. 20036-4688

ISBN: 0-7922-6071-6

Third Printing 2007
Printed in China

Contents

Look at this bulletin board.
What is this class learning about?

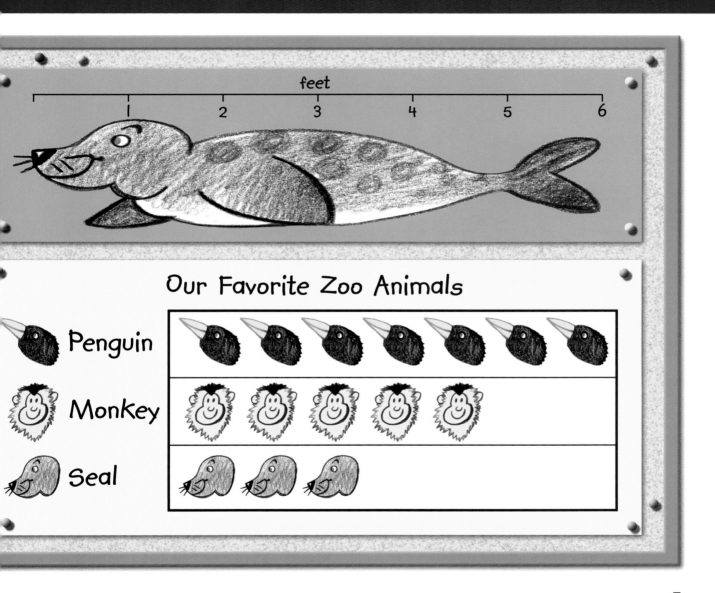

Data

Data is information.
You can count to collect data.
You can measure and weigh to collect data.

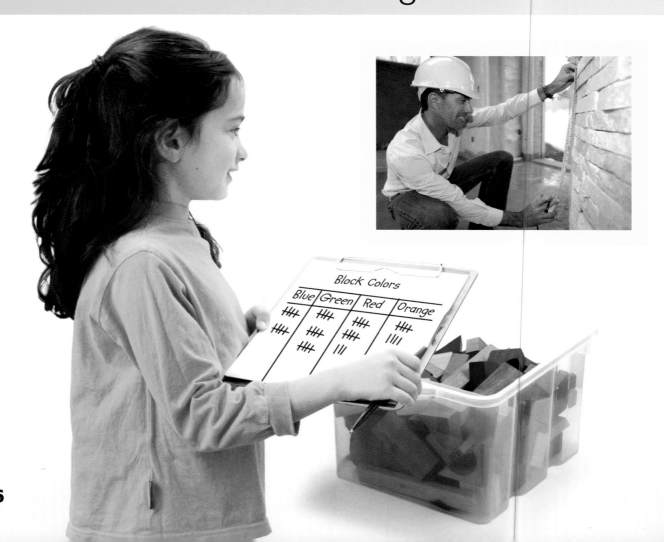

Block Colors

Blue	Green	Red	Orange

Height and Length

You can measure height and length.

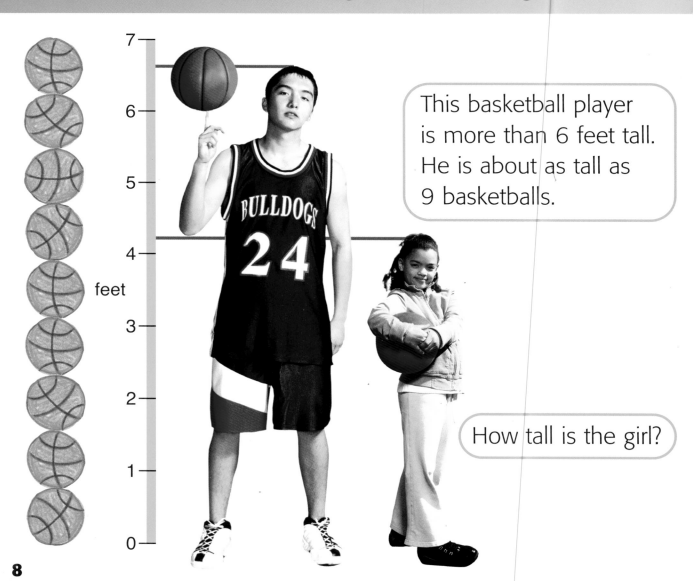

This basketball player is more than 6 feet tall. He is about as tall as 9 basketballs.

How tall is the girl?

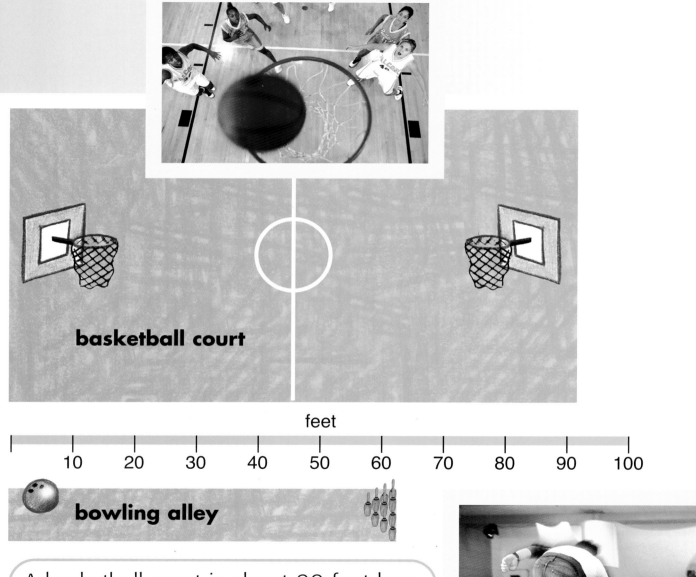

basketball court

feet

| | | | | | | | | | |
|10|20|30|40|50|60|70|80|90|100|

bowling alley

A basketball court is about 90 feet long.
About how long is a bowling alley?

Weight

You can weigh things.
Sometimes we weigh food.

The watermelon weighs about 10 pounds.

The watermelon weighs about as much as 10 loaves of bread.

Counting

You can count to collect data.
You can show the data in a graph.

What's Your Favorite Fruit?

orange	apple	banana
⑉⑉ ||	⑉⑉	||||

The teacher is counting.

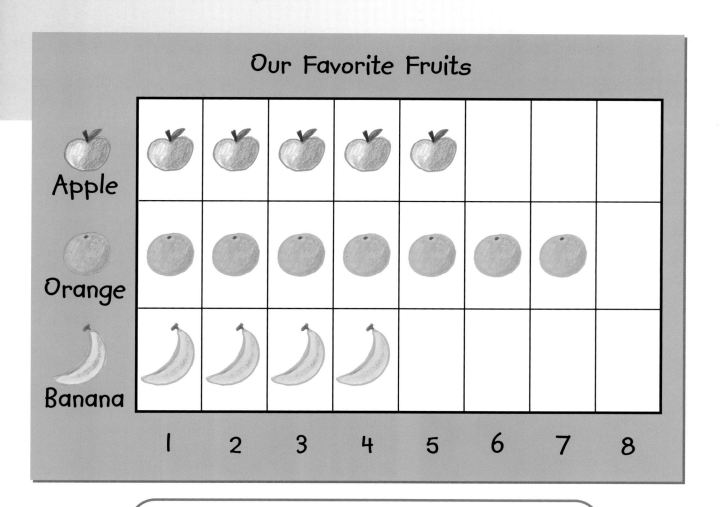

Our Favorite Fruits

This picture graph shows favorite fruits.
Do more children like bananas or apples?
Which fruit do most children like the best?

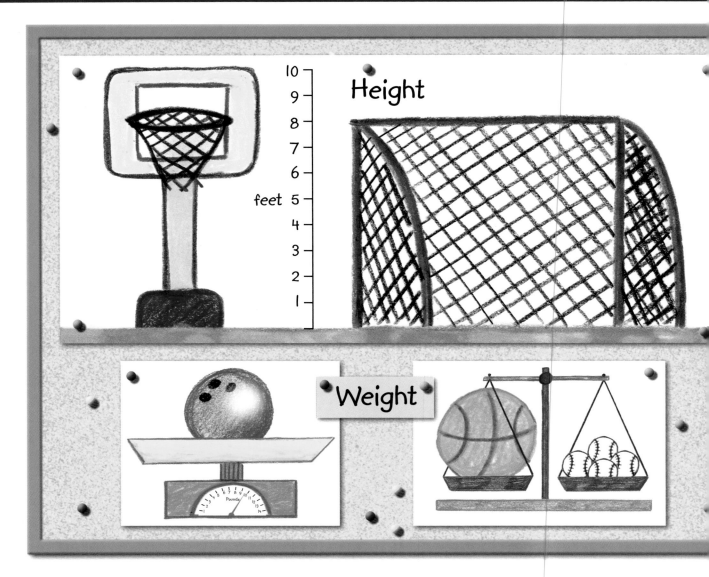

Height

feet

Weight

Look at this data.
What does it tell you?

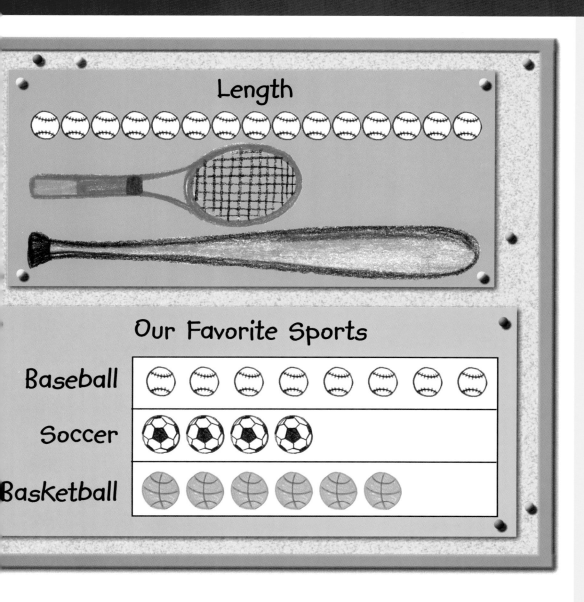

Length

Our Favorite Sports

Baseball	⚾ ⚾ ⚾ ⚾ ⚾ ⚾ ⚾ ⚾
Soccer	⚽ ⚽ ⚽ ⚽
Basketball	🏀 🏀 🏀 🏀 🏀 🏀

data

feet (foot)

graph

long

measure

pounds

tall

weigh

Picture Glossary

count

height

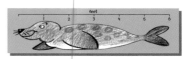

length

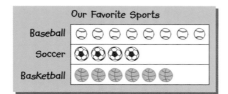

picture graph

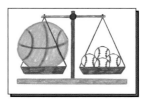

weight

16